Jokes Your
Minister Can Tell

Compiled by
Israel Galindo

Jokes Your Minister Can Tell
Copyright © 2017, Israel Galindo. All rights reserved.
This material may not be photocopied or reproduced
in any way without written permission of the publisher
or author.

Published by Didache Press

Contents

Introduction

As part of his talk at a gala banquet honoring top city officials and attended by the shakers and movers of the city, a minister told some jokes and a few funny stories. Since he planned to use the same anecdotes at a meeting the next day, he asked reporters covering the event not to include them in their articles.

Reading the paper the following morning, he noticed that one well-meaning reporter had ended his story about the banquet with the observation "The minister told a number of stories that cannot be published."

I'll confess I'm one of those persons who is not good at telling jokes, but I appreciate humor and good stories that tickle the frontal lobe. A recent study on humor found that the most enduring jokes over the course of history tend to be on the more baser subjects (think fart jokes). Unfortunately, you can't tell fart jokes to your pastor, even if privately, your minister likely knows more of those than you.

Here is a collection of jokes you can tell your minister. Or, if you need, a resource of jokes your minister can use if she or he needs a new supply of pulpit jokes.

Hearing

"What's wrong, Bubba?" asked the pastor.

"I need you to pray for my hearing," said Bubba.

The pastor put his hands on Bubba's ears and prayed. When he was done, he asked, "So how's your hearing?"

"I don't know," said Bubba. "my hearing isn't until next Tuesday."

Lawn Mower

Gary was having a yard sale. A minister bought a lawn mower but returned it a few days later, complaining that it wouldn't run.

"It'll run," said Gary. "But you have to curse at it to get it started."

The minister took umbrage and complained. "I have not uttered a curse in 30 years."

"Just keep pulling on the starter rope—the words will come back to you."

The Sign

A priest and a pastor are standing by the side of a road holding up a sign that reads "The end is near! Turn around now before it's too late!"

A passing driver yells, "You guys are nuts!" and speeds past them. From around the curve, they hear screeching tires—then a big splash.

The priest turns to the pastor and says, "Do you think we should just put up a sign that says 'Bridge Out' instead?"

Saint Peter

Two doctors and an HMO manager die and line up together at the Pearly Gates. One doctor steps forward and tells St. Peter, "As a pediatric surgeon, I saved hundreds of children." St. Peter lets him enter.

The next doctor says, "As a psychiatrist, I helped thousands of people live better lives." St. Peter tells him to go ahead.

The last man says, "I was an HMO manager. I got countless families cost-effective health care."

St. Peter replies, "You may enter. But," he adds, "you can only stay for three days. After that, you can go to hell."

Healing

Three guys are fishing when an angel appears.

The first guy says, "I've suffered from back pain for years. Can you help me?" The angel touches the man's back, and he feels instant relief.

The second guy points to his thick glasses and begs for a cure for his poor eyesight. When the angel tosses the lenses into the lake, the man gains 20/20 vision.

As the angel turns to the third man, he instantly recoils and screams, "Don't touch me! I'm on disability!"

Gandhi

Gandhi walked barefoot everywhere, ate very little, and often fasted, leaving him thin and with very bad breath. Thus he is often thought of as a super callused, fragile mystic plagued with halitosis.

Seattle

Howard dies and waits in line for judgment. He notices that some souls go right into heaven, while Satan throws others into a burning pit. But every so often, instead of hurling a poor soul into the fire, the devil tosses it aside.

Curious, Howard asks Satan, "Excuse me, but why are you tossing them aside instead of flinging them into hell with the others?"

"They're from Seattle," Satan replies. "They're too wet to burn."

One Wish

An angel appears at a faculty meeting and tells the dean, "In return for your unselfish and exemplary behavior, the Lord will reward you with your choice of infinite wealth, wisdom, or beauty."

"Give me infinite wisdom!" declares the dean, without hesitation.

"Done!" says the angel before disappearing in a cloud of smoke.

All heads now turn to the dean, who sits surrounded by a faint halo of light. "Well," says a colleague, "say something brilliant."

The dean stands and, with the poise of Socrates, opines, "I should have taken the money."

Commandments

When I asked my friend if she was planning to attend church, she just shook her head. "I haven't gone in a long time," she said. "Besides, it's too late for me. I've probably already broken all seven commandments."

Denomination

A woman goes to the post office and asks for 50 Hanukkah stamps.

"What denomination?" asks the clerk.

The woman says, "Six Orthodox, 12 Conservative, and 32 Reform."

Doctor

A doctor died and went to heaven, where he found a long line at St. Peter's gate. As was his custom, the doctor rushed to the front, but St. Peter told him to wait in line like everyone else. Muttering and looking at his watch, the doctor stood at the end of the line.

Moments later a white-haired man wearing a white coat and carrying a stethoscope and medical bag rushed up to the front of the line, waved to St. Peter, and was immediately admitted through the Pearly Gates.

"Hey!" the doctor shouted. "How come you let him through?"

"Oh," said St. Peter, "that's God. Sometimes he likes to play doctor."

Babies

A child asked his father, "How were people born?" So his father said, "Adam and Eve made babies, then their babies became adults and made babies, and so on."

The child then went to his mother, asked her the same question and she told him, "We were monkeys then we evolved to become like we are now."

The child ran back to his father and said, "You lied to me!"

His father replied, "No, your mom was talking about her side of the family

Marriage

With Bible in hand, I read to my high school religion class, "For this cause shall a man leave his father and mother, and cleave to his wife."

"Okay," I said, "from this Scripture, what do we learn is important in marriage?"

A student blurted out, "Cleavage."

Casket

The pastor asks his flock, "What would you like people to say when you're in your casket?"

One congregant says, "I'd like them to say I was a fine family man."

Another says, "I'd like them to say I helped people."

The third responds, "I'd like them to say, 'Look! I think he's moving!' "

Horse

A preacher trained his horse to go when he said, "Praise the Lord," and to stop when he said, "Amen." The preacher mounted the horse, said, "Praise the Lord" and went for a ride. When he wanted to stop for lunch, he said, "Amen." He took off again, saying, "Praise the Lord." The horse started going toward the edge of a cliff. The preacher got excited and said, "Whoa!" Then he remembered and said, "Amen," and the horse stopped at the edge of the cliff.

The preacher was so relieved and grateful that he looked up to heaven and said, "Praise the Lord!"

Donation

The phone rings at the synagogue office.

"Hello, is this Rabbi Schwartz?" The caller asked.

"It is."

"This is the Internal Revenue Service. We wonder if you can help us."

"I'll try."

"Do you know Herman Cohen?"

"I do."

"Is this man a member of your congregation."

"He is."

"Did he donate $10,000?"

"He will."

Lying

As a pastor is wrapping up his service, he tells his congregation "Next week I will deliver a sermon on the evils of lying. To prepare for it, I would like you all to read Mark chapter 17."

The next week in service he asks how many parishioners read the 17th chapter of Mark.

Every hand in the congregation goes up. "Mark has only 16 chapters," the pastor continues with a grin. "I will now proceed with the sermon on lying."

Hospital Visit

Old Deacon Roberts had been a faithful Christian and was in the hospital, near death. The family called their pastor to stand with them. As the pastor stood next to the bed, deacon Robert's condition appeared to deteriorate and he motioned frantically for something to write on.

The pastor lovingly handed him a pen and a piece of paper, and deacon Roberts used his last bit of energy to scribble a note, then he died.

The pastor thought it best not to look at the note at that time, so he placed it in his jacket pocket.

At the funeral, as he was finishing the message, he realized that he was wearing the same jacket that he was wearing when Ol' Fred died. He said, "You know, deacon Roberts handed me a note just before he died. I haven't looked at it, but knowing Fred, I'm sure there's a word of inspiration there for us all."

He opened the note, and read, "You're standing on my oxygen tube!"

Missed Again

The preacher and his friend had teed off. The friend missed a short putt for his birdie and swore under his breath. At the third hole, he missed another easy putt. "Damn! Missed again," he muttered.

On the seventh hole, he did it again. "Damn! Another miss!" he groaned. The preacher kept giving his friend reproachful glances but said nothing. They started out on the back nine.

On the tenth hole, the ball just missed the cup. "Damn! Missed again!"

"Look!" cried the preacher. "I'm tired of your swearing. If you do it again, I'm going to call on the Lord to strike you."

Yeah, yeah, thought the friend as he teed off on the eleventh. The rest of his putts were accurate until the last hole, where a two-meter putt rolled up to the lip of the cup and stopped right there. "Damn, damn, damn! Missed again!"

A huge black cloud formed overhead and rolled around for a few seconds. Then a lightning bolt whizzed down from the sky and zapped the preacher.

The friend gaped in amazement as the clouds opened up and disappeared. Then a sepulchral voice came from nowhere: "Damn! Missed again!"

Prescription

When a local doctor began attending church services the minister was delighted, and it wasn't long before they were helping each other in their work, the minister referring people to the doctor, and vice versa.

One referral from the doctor called at the church office with a note prescribing the minister's last four sermons. The minister was most pleased until he discovered that the patient's problem was insomnia.

17

Golf

The new parish priest was invited to play golf with two friends. Although he admitted his game was terrible, he went along anyway.

At the first tee, another golfer joined them to make a foursome. So as not to make the stranger nervous, the priest insisted they introduce him as "Ron."

On the fourth hole, the other golfer turned to Ron and asked him what he did for a living. Confronted, Ron admitted that he was a Catholic priest. "I knew it!" the stranger exclaimed. "The way you play golf and don't swear, you'd have to be a priest."

Keeping Confidence

Sue, and her husband, Andrew, an Anglican priest were being interviewed by the search committee for a new pastor for a church in a small town.

At one point, the question of the prospective priest's ability to keep a confidence arose.

A member of the committee turned to Sue and asked, "If one of our women parishioners went to your husband for advice about her husband's infidelity with another woman, would you know about it?"

Sue promptly answered, "Only if I were the other woman." Andrew received the appointment.

Wrong Way

The pastor of the church was a shocked and dismayed that Mrs. Wendell, the biggest donor, had just made her first parachute jump with a sky-divers club.

He scolded me for doing such a "crazy thing."

"But," said Mrs. Wendell, "I'm so close to heaven up there."

"Yes," the pastor replied trying to dissuade her, "but you're going the wrong way!"

Last Request

Father O'Grady was saying his goodbye's to the parishioners after his Sunday morning service as he always does when Mary Clancey came up to him in tears.

"What's bothering you so, dear?" inquired Farther O'Grady.

"Oh, father, I've got terrible news." Replied Mary. "Well what is it, Mary?"

"Well, my husband, passed away last night, Father."

"Oh, Mary" said the father, "that's terrible. Tell me Mary, did he have any last requests?"

"Well, yes he did father," replied Mary.

"What did he ask, Mary?"

Mary replied, "He said, 'Please, Mary, put down the gun!"

Chapter and Verse

Pastor Steve was new in town and went out one Saturday to visit his parishioners. All went well until he came to one house. It was obvious that someone was home, but no one came to the door even after he had knocked several times.

Finally, he took out his card, wrote on the back "Revelation 3:20 " and stuck it in the door.

The next day, as he was counting the offering he found his card in the collection plate. Below his message was notation "Genesis 3:10."

Revelation 3:20 reads: "Behold, I stand at the door and knock. If any man hear my voice, and opens the door, I will come in to him, and will dine with him, and he with me."

Genesis 3:10 reads: "And he said, I heard thy voice in the garden, and I was afraid, because I was naked."

Dilemma

The Reverend Andrew woke up Sunday morning
and realizing it was an exceptionally beautiful
and sunny early spring day, decided he just had
to play golf, despite his overly responsible first-
born tendencies.

So, he told the Associate Pastor that he was
feeling sick and convinced him to say Mass for
him that day.

As soon as the Associate Pastor left the room,
Father Norton headed out of town to a golf
course about forty miles away. This way he
knew he wouldn't accidentally meet anyone he
knew from his parish.

Setting up on the first tee, he was alone. After
all, it was Sunday morning and everyone else
was in church!

At about this time, Saint Peter leaned over to
the Lord while looking down from the heavens
and exclaimed, "You're not going to let him get
away with this, are you?" The Lord sighed, and
said, "No, I guess not."

Just then Father Andrew hit the ball and it shot
straight towards the pin, dropping just short of
it, rolled up and fell into the hole. It Was a 420
Yard HOLE IN ONE!

St. Peter was astonished. He looked at the Lord
and asked, "Why did you let him do that?" The

Lord smiled and replied, "Who's he going to tell?"

Speeding

The minister was anxious to get home to his family after several days absence. He was traveling just over the speed limit when he was pulled up by a police officer who was unimpressed by the minister's explanation.

"A minister, eh? How would you like me to preach you a little sermon?"

"Skip the sermon," the minister replied with a sigh. "Just take up the collection."

The Hint

Mrs. Grady grew increasingly impatient with the length of the new young pastor's sermon. Being on the considerate side she was hesitant to broach the subject with the young minister lest she hurt his feelings.

One Sunday morning she asked the minister, "And what is the subject of your sermon this morning?"

"The milk of human kindness," replied the young minister.

"Condensed, I hope," replied Mrs. Grady.

The Barber

A rabbi got his haircut and was ready to pay the barber. The barber said "No rabbi, no charge for clergy here." The following morning the barber found a nice loaf of Jewish rye bread on his doorstep.

The next day the barber was cutting the hair of a Catholic priest. Again, he told the priest, "No charge to clergy." The following morning the barber found a bottle of wine on his steps.

On the next day, the barber gave a Baptist minister a haircut and told him the same thing, "No charge to the clergy."

The following morning the barber found 15 Baptist ministers on his doorstep.

Gideon

Two friends from college days met after many, many years. One of them had always been very ambitious and had become quite successful after years of hard work. The other man was not ambitious at all.

The ambitious man asked the other guy how he was doing. The other man replied, "Oh, great!! I opened my Bible and placed my finger on a word and it said oil, so I invested in oil. Boy, did those wells pay out! Then I placed my finger on another word and it said gold. Those mines are sure doing great!"

The ambitious man ran back to his hotel room and got the Gideon Bible, placed his finger on a word, and it said Chapter Eleven.

Stewardship

The regular organist had to take some time off, and a temporary organist was found for Sunday's service. The pastor gave her a list of hymns for the service, but said he had to make an unexpected announcement about finances, and the organist would have to think of something to play after that on her own.

During the announcements in the service, the pastor proceeded to tell the congregation that they needed $22,000 more to complete the church roof repairs.

He asked anyone willing to donate $1000 to please stand up. Just then the organist started to play "The Star Spangled Banner" and everyone stood up! And that is how the temporary organist became the new permanent organist.

Sharing

A mother was making pancakes for her sons, Douglas, 5, and Thomas, 3. The boys began to argue over who would get the first pancake. Their mother saw the opportunity for a moral lesson. "If Jesus were sitting here," she told them, "he would say, 'Let my brother have the first pancake. I can wait.'"

So Douglas turned to his younger brother and said, "Thomas, you be Jesus!"

Helping

A pastor was walking down the street and saw a young boy trying very hard to reach a doorbell to ring it. As he watched the young boy struggle, the pastor went up on the porch, reached over the boy and rang the doorbell for him.

Then the pastor asked, "And now what, young man?" The little boy replied, "And now we run!"

Haircut

The young minister's son had just gotten his driving permit. He asked his father if they could discuss his use of the car.

"I'll make a deal with you," said his father. "You bring your grades up, study your Bible a little, get your hair cut, and then we'll talk."

A month later the boy came back and again asked his father if they could discuss his use of the car.

"Son, I'm real proud of you. You've brought your grades up and you've studied your Bible, but you didn't get hair cut!"

"You know, Dad, I've been thinking about that. Samson had long hair, Moses had long hair,

Noah had long hair, and even Jesus had long hair."

"Yes son, and they walked everywhere they went!"

Forbearance

A man became fed up with humanity and decided to spend the rest of his life in a monastery. The abbot warned him that he would have to take a vow of silence and live a life of obedience. The man replied, "No problem. I'm sick of talking."

Ten years went by, and the abbot called for the man. He told him that he was model monk and they were very happy with him. As per tradition he was allowed say two words. So he nodded and said, "Food cold." The abbot sent him on his way.

Ten years later, he was brought before the abbot again and told how pleased they were with his performance, and he was again allowed two more words. The man said, "Bed hard," and was sent back to work.

Another ten years went by and again the abbot sent for the man, telling him he was the best monk they had ever had, and that he was allowed another two words. The man nodded and said, "I quit."

Abbot replied in a disgusted tone, "Doesn't surprise me. You're done nothing but complain since you got here."

Entering Heaven

A minister dies and is waiting in line at the Pearly Gates. Ahead of him is a guy who's dressed in sunglasses, a loud shirt, leather jacket, and jeans.

Saint Peter addresses this guy, "Who are you, so that I may know whether or not to admit you to the Kingdom of Heaven?"

The guy replies, "I'm Joe Cohen, taxi driver, of Noo Yawk City."

St. Peter consults his list. He smiles and says to the taxi driver, "Take this silken robe and golden staff and enter the Kingdom of Heaven."

The taxi driver goes into Heaven with his robe and staff, and it's the minister's turn. He stands erect and booms out, "I am Joseph Snow, pastor of Calvary for the last forty-three years."

St Peter consults his list. He says to the minister, "Take this cotton robe and wooden staff and enter the Kingdom of Heaven."

"Just a minute," says the minister. "That man was a taxi driver, and he gets a silken robe and golden staff. How can this be?"

"Up here, we consider the results of your work," says Saint Peter. "While you preached, people slept; while he drove, people prayed."

Graveside

A funeral director asked the new young minister in town to hold a grave side service for a homeless man with no family or friends. The graveside service was to be at a cemetery way out in the country. This was a new cemetery and this man was the first to be laid to rest there, explained the funeral director.

Not being familiar with the area the new minister became lost. Being a typical man he did not ask for directions and finally found the cemetery about an hour late. The back hoe was there and the crew was eating their lunch. The hearse was nowhere to be seen.

The young minister apologized to the workers for being late. As he looked into the open grave, he saw the vault lid already in place. He told the workers I would not keep them long, but that this was the proper thing to do. The workers, still eating their lunch, gathered around the opening.

Being young and enthusiastic he poured out my heart and soul as he preached the graveside sermon. The workers joined in with, "Praise the Lord," "Amen," and "Glory!" He got so into the service that he preached and preached and preached, from Genesis to The Revelation.

When the service was over, he said a prayer and walked to his car, satisfied with his performance.

As he got in his care he heard one of the workers say, "I never saw anything like that before and I've been putting in septic systems for twenty years."

New Church

A rich man went to his vicar and said, "I want you and your wife to take a three-month trip to the Holy Land at my expense. When you come back, I'll have a surprise for you". The vicar accepted the offer, and he and his wife went off to the Middle East.

Three months later they returned home and were met by the wealthy parishioner, who told them that while they were gone, he had had a new church built. "It's the finest building money can buy, vicar," said the man. "No expense was spared." And he was right. It was a magnificent edifice both outside and in.

But there was one striking difference. There was only one pew, and it was at the very back. "A church with only one pew?" asked the vicar.

"You just wait until Sunday," the rich man said.

When the time came for the Sunday service, the early arrivals entered the church, filed onto the one pew and sat down. When the pew was full, a switch clicked silently, a circuit closed, the gears meshed, a belt moved and, automatically, the rear pew began to move forward. When it reached the front of the church, it came to a stop. At the same time, another empty pew came up from below at the back and more people sat down. And so it continued, pews filling and moving forwards until finally the church was full, from front to back.

"Wonderful!" said the vicar, "Marvelous!"

The service began, and the vicar started to preach his sermon. He launched into his text and, when 12 o'clock came, he was still going strong, with no end in sight. Suddenly a bell rang, and a trap door in the floor behind the pulpit dropped open.

"Wonderful!" said the congregation, "Marvelous!"

The Barber

Steve the barber was a new convert. He was filled with enthusiasm and eager to share his new faith. He thought he should share his faith with his customers and he had the evangelistic zeal to do it. The next morning when the sun came up and the barber got up out of bed he said, "Today I am going to witness to the first man that walks through my door."

Soon after Steve opened his shop the first man came in and said, "I want a shave!" The barber said, "Sure, just sit in the seat and I'll be with you in a moment."

The barber went in the back and prayed a quick desperate prayer saying, "God, the first customer came in and I'm going to witness to him. Give me the wisdom to know just the right thing to say to him. Amen."

Then the barber came out with his razor knife in one hand and a Bible in the other while saying "Good morning sir. I have a question for you... Are you ready to die?"

The Interview

The young country preacher was interviewing for a call to a very rural church. The committee chairman asked, "Son, do you know the Bible pretty good?"

The young minister said, "Yes, pretty good." The chairman asked, "Which part do you know best?" He responded saying, "I know the New Testament best."

"Which part of the New Testament do you know best," asked the chairman. The young minister said, "Several parts."

The chairman said, "Well, why don't you tell us the story of the Prodigal Son." The young man said, "Fine."

"There was a man of the Pharisees name Nicodemus, who went down to Jericho by night and he fell upon stony ground and the thorns choked him half to death.

"The next morning Solomon and his wife, Gomorrah, came by, and carried him down to the ark for Moses to take care of. But, as he was going through the Eastern Gate into the Ark, he caught his hair in a limb and he hung there forty days and forty nights and he afterwards did hunger. And, the ravens came and fed him.

"The next day, the three wise men came and carried him down to the boat dock and he caught a ship to Nineveh. And when he got there he found Delilah sitting on the wall. He said, "Chunk her down, boys, chunk her down." And, they said, "How many times shall we chunk her down, till seven time seven?" And he said, "Nay, but seventy times seven." And they chucked her down four hundred and ninety times.

"And, she burst asunder in their midst. And they picked up twelve baskets of the leftovers. And, in the resurrection whose wife shall she be?"

The Committee chairman thanked the young preacher and asked him to step outside so the committee could deliberate.

"Fellows, I think we ought to ask the church to call him as our minister," said the chairman, "He is awfully young, but he sure does know his Bible."

Answered Prayer

A flood was on its way, forcing everyone to evacuate. The police rowed up to the most pious woman in town and said, "Ma'am, you have to leave this house! People are dying out here!"

The woman replied, "No, I'm not leaving. God has always helped me before, and He will do it again."

So as the water started to rise, she went to the second story of her house. Another boat came by, and the captain yelled, "Ma'am, you have to get on this boat or you're going to drown!"

The woman replied again, "No, God helped me before, and He will do it again."

The water rose even higher. This time she went to the top of the roof, where a helicopter came and hovered overhead. The pilot called into his loudspeaker, "Please climb aboard, ma'am. You are going to drown!"

The women sniffed and again replied, "God is going to save me!"

But the water rose higher, and soon she drowned to death. She went to Heaven, and there she asked God, "Why didn't you save me, O Lord?"

And God replied, "I did help—I sent you two boats and a helicopter!"

Pastoral Advice

For the umpteenth time Mrs. Frederick came to her pastor to tell him, "I'm so scared! Joe says he's going to kill me if I continue to come to your church."

"Yes, yes, my child," replied the pastor, more than a little tired of hearing this over and over. "I will continue to pray for you, Mrs. Frederick. Have faith, Lord will watch over you."

"Oh yes, he has kept me safe thus far, only....."

"Only what, my child?"

"Well, now he says if I keep coming to your church, he's going to kill YOU!"

"Well, now," said the pastor, "Perhaps it's time to check out that little church on the other side of town."

Faith

A man named Jack was walking along a steep cliff one day, when he accidentally got too close to the edge and fell. On the way down he grabbed a branch, which temporarily stopped his fall. He looked down and to his horror saw that the canyon fell straight down for more than a thousand feet.

He couldn't hang onto the branch forever, and there was no way for him to climb up the steep wall of the cliff. So Jack began yelling for help, hoping that someone passing by would hear him and lower a rope or something.

"HELP! HELP! Is anyone up there? "HELP!"

He yelled for a long time, but no one heard him. He was about to give up when he heard a voice. Jack, Jack. Can you hear me?"

"Yes, yes! I can hear you. I'm down here!"

"I can see you, Jack. Are you all right?"

"Yes, but who are you, and where are you?

"I am the Lord, Jack. I'm everywhere."

"The Lord? You mean, GOD?"

"That's Me."

"God, please help me! I promise if, you'll get me down from here, I'll stop sinning. I'll be a really good person. I'll serve You for the rest of my life."

"Easy on the promises, Jack. Let's get you off from there; then we can talk. Now, here's what I want you to do. Listen carefully."

"I'll do anything, Lord. Just tell me what to do."

"Okay. Let go of the branch."

"What?" "I said, let go of the branch?!"

"Just trust Me. Let go."

There was a long silence.

Finally Jack yelled, "HELP! HELP! IS ANYONE ELSE UP THERE?"

Effort

Dan finds himself in dire trouble. His business has gone bust and he's in serious financial trouble. He's so desperate that he decides to ask God for help.

He begins to pray, "God, please help me. I've lost my business and if I don't get some money, I'm going to lose my house as well. Please let me win the lotto."

Lotto night comes and somebody else wins it.

Dan again prays, "God, please let me win the lotto! I've lost my business, my house and I'm going to lose my car as well".

Lotto night comes and Dan still has no luck.

Once again, he prays in desperation, "My God, why have you forsaken me?? I've lost my business, my house, and my car. My wife and children are starving. I don't often ask you for help and I have always been a good servant to you. PLEASE just let me win the lotto this one time so I can get my life back in order."

Suddenly there is a blinding flash of light as the heavens open and Joe is confronted by the voice of God Himself:

"Dan, meet Me halfway on this. Buy a ticket."

Bricks

There was a very rich man who was just about to die and he wanted to take some of his wealth with him. So he started negotiations with God about the matter. God was not sure as it had never been done before and he did not want to set a precedence. Finally after long talks God reluctantly agreed to allow him to bring his wealth to heaven.

Just a few days before he died the rich man converted all his money into gold bullion. He died and the funeral home made sure that the suitcases containing the gold bullion went with him. He arrived at the Pearly Gates with his suitcases and there was Peter. Peter told him he could not bring the suitcases into heaven. But the man said he had already spoken to God and he had said it was OK.

So Peter got on the God phone and sure enough it was true. So Peter was curious as to what was so valuable that the man wanted to bring it into heaven. Peter said, "Could I look in the suitcases?"

So the man opened the suitcases and Peter exclaimed, "Why are you bringing pavement to heaven!"

Contractor

Three contractors were touring the Manse on the same day. One was from New York, another from Missouri, and the third from Florida. At the end of the tour, the priest asked them what they did for a living. When they each replied that they were contractors, the priest said, "Hey we need one of the rear fences redone. Why don't you men take a look at it and give me your bids."

First, the Florida contractor took out his tape measure and pencil, did some measuring and said, "I figure the job will run about $900: $400 for materials, $400 for my crew, and $100 profit for me."

Next was the Missouri contractor. He also took out his tape measure and pencil, did some quick calculations and said, "Looks like I can do this job for $700: $300 for materials, $300 for my crew, and $100 profit for me."

Finally, the priest asks the New York contractor for his bid. Without batting an eye, the contractor says, "$2,700."

The priest, incredulous, looks at him and says, "You didn't even measure like the others! How did you come up with such a high figure?"

Easy," says the contractor from New York, "$1,000 for me, $1,000 for you, and we hire the guy from Missouri."

Cooking

Two cannibals meet one day. The first cannibal says, "You know, I just can't seem to get a tender Missionary. I've baked them, I've roasted them, I've stewed them, I've barbecued them, I've tried every sort of marinade. I just cannot seem to get them tender."

The second cannibal asks, "What kind of Missionary do you use?" The other replied, "You know, the ones that hang out at that place at the bend of the river. They have those brown cloaks with a rope around the waist and they're sort of bald on top with a funny ring of hair on their heads."

"Ah, I see what the your problem is," the second cannibal replies. "No wonder, those are friars!"

Insult

A woman got on a bus holding a baby. The bus driver said: "That's the ugliest baby I've ever seen." In a huff, the woman slammed her fare into the fare box and took an aisle seat near the rear of the bus.

The minister seated next to her sensed that she was agitated and in his most practiced pastoral care voice asked her what was wrong.

"The bus driver insulted me," she fumed.

The minister sympathized and said: "Why, he's a public servant and shouldn't say things to insult passengers."

"You're right," she said. "I think I'll go back up there and give him a piece of my mind."

"That's a good idea," the minister said. "Here, let me hold your monkey."

Jerks

One afternoon, Pastor Bob drives down a highway to visit a nearby lake and relax. On his way to the lake, a guy dressed from head to toe in red standing on the side of the highway gestures for him to stop.

Pastor Bob rolls down the window and says, "How can I help you?"

"I am the red jerk of the highway. You got something to eat?"

With a smile on his face, the pastor hands a sandwich to the guy in red and drives away. Not even five minutes later, he comes across another guy. This guy is dressed fully in yellow, standing on the side of the road and waving for him to stop.

A bit irritated, Pastor Bob stops, cranks down the window, and says, "What can I do for you?"

"I am the yellow jerk of the highway. You got something to drink?"

Hardly managing to smile this time, Pastor Bob hands the guy a can of Coke and stomps on the pedal and takes off again. In order to make it to the lakeside before sunset, he decides to go faster and not to stop no matter what.

To his frustration, he sees another guy on the side of the road, this one dressed in blue and signaling for him to stop. Reluctantly, Pastor Bob decides to stop one last time.

He rolls down his window, and yells, "Let me guess. You're the blue jerk of the highway, and just what the heck do you wanna have?"

"Driver's license and registration, please."

Dinner

Pastor James was delighted with the way the painter had done all the work on the manse. "You did a great job." he said and handed the man a check. "Also, in order to thank you, here's an extra $80 to take the missus out to dinner and a movie."

Later that night, the doorbell rang and it was the painter. Thinking the man had forgotten something Pastor James asked, "What's the matter, did you forget something?"

"Nope." replied the painter. "I'm just here to take your missus out to dinner and a movie like you asked."

Salute

Deacon Gary was a retired military man who was very patriotic. He had a tall flag in his front yard. One day he talked with a Jehovah Witness and got very upset when he found out the Jehovah's Witnesses refused to serve in the armed services, to say the pledge of allegiance, or to salute the flag.

He decided that he would talk not to any more Jehovah's Witnesses unless they were willing to salute the flag and say the pledge of allegiance. One day he was sitting in his living room looking out the window when he saw a Jehovah's Witness with her little girl walking towards his front door. When she knocked at the door he was ready for her.

He opened the door and before she could open her mouth he told her, "I'm not going to talk with you or listen to what you say unless you turn, face that flag in my front yard, salute it and say the pledge of allegiance!"

The woman looked very confused, but she finally turned, faced the flag, saluted, and said the pledge of allegiance.

Deacon Gary was just shocked by what he witnessed. He turned to the lady and said, "You know, you're the first Jehovah's Witness I have ever met who would salute the flag and say the pledge of allegiance!"

The woman, with a confused look on her face replied, "Jehovah's Witness? I'm the Avon Lady!"

Eyesight

Pastor Gordon's wife and congregants were getting worried about his failing eyesight. Their cause for concerned was confirmed one day when pastor Gordon was driving down the freeway on the way to church.

As he was driving his cell phone rang. Answering, he heard his wife's voice urgently warning him, "Gordon, I just heard on the news that there's a car going the wrong way on Highway 401. Please be careful!"

"Darn it," said pastor Gordon, "It's not just one car. It's hundreds of them!"

Language Barrier

The new missionary recruit went to Venezuela for the first time. He was struggling with the language and didn't understand a whole lot of what was going on. Intending to visit one of the local churches, he got lost, but eventually got back on track and found the place.

Having arrived late, the church was already packed. The only pew left was the one on the front row.

So as not to make a fool of himself, he decided to pick someone out of the crowd to imitate. He chose to follow the man sitting next to him on the front pew. As they sang, the man clapped his hands, so the missionary recruit clapped too.

When the man stood up to pray, the missionary recruit stood up too. When the man sat down, he sat down. When the man held the cup and bread for the Lord's Supper, he held the cup and bread.

During the preaching, the recruit didn't understand a thing. He just sat there and tried to look just like that man in the front pew.

Then he perceived that the preacher was giving announcements. People clapped, so he looked to see if the man was clapping. He was, and so the recruit clapped too.

Then the preacher said some words that he didn't understand and he saw the man next to him stand up. So he stood up too. Suddenly a hush fell over the entire congregation. A few people gasped. He looked around and saw that nobody else was standing. So he sat down.

After the service ended, the preacher stood at the door shaking the hands of those who were leaving. When the missionary recruit stretched out his hand to greet the preacher, the preacher said, in English: "I take it you don't speak Spanish."

The missionary recruit replied: "No I don't. It's that obvious?"

"Well yes," said the preacher, "I announced that the Acosta family had a newborn baby boy and would the proud father please stand up."

Quick Thinking

The sharp new clerk at the supermarket was assigned to the produce section. A customer asked him if she could buy half a grapefruit. Not knowing what to do, he excused himself to ask the manager.

"Some nut out there wants to buy half a grapefruit..." he began, and, suddenly realizing that the customer had entered the office behind him, continued, " ... and this lovely lady would like to buy the other half."

The manager was impressed with the way the clerk amicably resolved the problem and they later started chatting. "Where are you from?" asked the store manager.

"Lancaster, Pennsylvania," replied the clerk, "home of ugly women and great hockey teams."

"Oh, my *WIFE* is from Lancaster," challenged the manager.

Without skipping a beat, the clerk asked, "What team was she on?"

Hearing

Nick had fallen on hard times. He lost his job at the fertilizer plant, his wife had left him, his unemployment had run out, and he was evicted from his apartment. He packed what little he had in a knapsack, made a little sign that read

"Will work for food" and set off down the road on foot.

Toward the middle of the day, he came to a parsonage. He was getting very hungry, and so he knocked on the front door, figuring a minister would show compassion. The minister's wife answered, and Leroy explained his situation, and how he could do most anything and how hungry he was.

At first the woman wanted no part of Leroy, but he persisted. Finally she asked "Can you paint?"

"Oh yes, ma'am," Leroy said, "I sure can paint. I've done a lot of painting. Just let me show you." The minister's wife relented, found a can of paint and a brush and said, "You go around back and paint the porch, and I'll fix you dinner." Happily, Leroy went to work.

About 40 minutes later, Nick appeared at the front door. "Are you finished so soon?" asked the woman.

"Oh yes, ma'am," said Nick, "but I think you ought to know that's not a Porsche, it's a Volvo."

The Interview Test

Two recent seminary graduates, Andy and Beth, applied for the same church call. Both applicants had the same qualifications and were equally impressive. The search committee was having a hard time deciding between the candidates, so they decided to give a written exam to determine who would receive the call.

Upon completion of the exam both candidates only missed one of the questions. The chair of the search committee went to Andy and said, "Thank you for your interest, but we've decided to give the position to Beth."

Andy replied, "Why? We both correctly answered nine questions. I believe I should get this job, especially since I've grown up in this town and Beth just moved here."

The chair of the search committee said, "We made our decision not on the correct answers, but on the question you missed."

"How could one incorrect answer be better than the other?," asked Andy.

"Simple," said the chair. "Beth put down on question number 5, 'I don't know', and you put down, 'Neither do I.'"

Sympathy

The Baptist preacher just finished his sermon for the day and proceeded toward the back of the church for his usual greetings and handshaking as the congregation left the church. After shaking a few adult hands he came upon the seven year old son of one of the Deacons of the church.

"Good morning, Jonathan," the preacher said as he reached out to shake Jonathan's hand.

As he was doing do he felt something in the palm of Jonathan's hand. "What's this?" the preacher asked.

"Money," said Jonathan with a big smile on his face, "It's for you!"

"I don't want to take your money, Jonathan," the preacher answered.

"I want you to have it," said Jonathan. After a short pause Jonathan continued, "My daddy says you're the poorest preacher we ever had and I want to help you."

The South

Seminarian Allan finally decided on a topic for his D.Min. project. He decided to write about churches around the country. He started by flying to San Francisco and working east from there.

He goes to a very large church and begins taking interviewing church members and staff and taking pictures. He spots a golden telephone on a wall and is intrigued with a sign which reads "$10,000.00 a minute." Seeking out the pastor, he asks about the phone and the sign. The pastor answers that this golden phone is, in fact, a direct line to Heaven, and if he pays the price he can talk directly to God. He thanks the pastor and continues on his way.

As he continues to visit churches in Seattle, Denver, Boise, Milwaukee, Chicago, New York, and on around the United States, he finds more phones with the same sign, and the same answer from each pastor.

Finally, he arrives in the South. Upon entering a church, lo and behold, he sees the usual golden telephone. But this time the sign reads "Calls: 25 cents." Fascinated, he asks to talk to the pastor.

"Reverend, I have been in cities all across the country and in each church I found this golden telephone, and I have been told it is a direct line to Heaven and that I could talk to God, but in the other churches the cost was $10,000.00 a minute. Your sign reads 25 cents a call. Why?"

The pastor, smiling, replies, "Son, you're in the South now. It's a local call."

Last Minute

The minister waited in line to have his car filled with gas just before a long holiday weekend. The attendant worked quickly, but there were many cars ahead of him in front of the service station. Finally, the attendant motioned him toward a vacant pump.

"Preacher," said the young man, "I'm sorry about the delay. It seems as if everyone waits until the last minute to get ready for a long trip."

49

The minister chuckled, "I know what you mean. It's the same in my business."

Mom

An elderly woman walked into the local country church. The friendly usher greeted her at the door and helped her up the flight of steps.

"Are you a first time visitor," asked the usher.

"Why yes, I am," replied the woman.

"Where would you like to sit?" he asked politely.

"The front row please." she answered.

"You really don't want to do that," the usher said. "The pastor is really boring."

"Do you happen to know who I am?" the woman inquired.

"No." he said.

"I'm the pastor's mother," she replied indignantly.

"Do you know who I am?" he asked.

"No." she said.

"Good", he answered.

Not Tempted

Pastor Terry was crossing a road one day when a frog called out to him and said, "If you kiss me, I'll turn into a beautiful princess." He bent over, picked up the frog and put it in his pocket.

The frog spoke up again and said, "If you kiss me and turn me back into a beautiful princess, I will stay with you for one week"

The pastor took the frog out of his pocket, smiled at it and returned it to the pocket.

The frog then cried out, "If you kiss me and turn me back into a princess, I'll stay with you and give you anything you want."

Again the pastor took the frog out, smiled at it and put it back into his pocket.

Finally, the frog asked, "What is the matter? I've told you I'm a beautiful princess, that I'll stay with you for a week and give you anything you want. Why won't you kiss me?"

The pastor said, "Look I'm a pastor. I already have a wife, but a talking frog, now that's cool!"

Lesson

Fred was teaching his first Sunday School lesson for the teen class. He wanted to make a good impression and make the lesson interesting, so he decided that a visual demonstration would add emphasis to Sunday's lesson. He placed four worms into four separate jars.

He put the first worm into a jar of alcohol.

He put the second worm into a jar of cigarette smoke.

He put the third worm into a jar of chocolate syrup.

He put the fourth worm into a jar of good clean soil.

At the conclusion of the lesson, Fred highlighted the following results:

The first worm in alcohol: Dead.

The second worm in cigarette smoke: Dead.

Third worm in chocolate syrup: Dead.

Fourth worm in good clean soil: Alive.

So Fred asked the class, "What can you learn from this demonstration?"

After some awkward silence, one teenager in the back shyly raised her hand and said, "As long as you drink, smoke and eat chocolate, you won't have worms?"

The Letter

A minister was opening his mail one morning. Drawing a single sheet of paper from an envelope, he found written on it only one word: "FOOL."

The next Sunday he announced, "I have known many people who have written letters and forgot to sign their names. But this week I received a letter from someone who signed his name but had forgotten to write a letter."

Motivation

One Sunday morning, a mother went in to wake her son and tell him it was time to get ready for church, to which he replied, "I'm not going."

"Why not?" she asked.

"I'll give you two good reasons," he said. "One, they don't like me, and two, I don't like them."

His mother replied, "I'll give YOU two good reasons why you SHOULD go to church. One, you're 54 years old, and two, you're the pastor!"

Confessions

Three pastors went to their denominational convention and were all sharing one room. The first pastor said, "Let's confess our secret sins one to another. I'll start. My secret sin is I just love to gamble. When I go out of town, it's cha-ching cha-ching, let the machines ring."

The second pastor said, "My secret sin is that I just hate working. I copy all my sermons from those given by other pastors."

The third pastor said, "My secret sin is gossiping and, oh boy, I just can't wait to get out of this room!"

Revival

After the revival had concluded, the three pastors were discussing the results with one another.

The Methodist minister said, "The revival worked out great for us! We gained four new families."

The Baptist preacher said, "We did better than that! We gained six new families."

The Presbyterian pastor said, "Well, we did even better than that! We got rid of our 10 biggest trouble makers!"

Eggs

Elderly pastor Elmer was searching his closet for his collar before church one Sunday morning. In the back of the closet, he found a small box containing 3 eggs and 100 $1 bills.

He called his wife into the closet to ask her about the box and its contents. Embarrassed, she admitted having hidden the box there for their entire 30 years of marriage. Disappointed and hurt, the pastor asked her, "WHY?"

Elmer's wife replied that she hadn't wanted to hurt his feelings. He asked her how the box could have hurt his feelings. She said that every time during their marriage that he had delivered a poor sermon, she had placed an egg in the box.

The pastor felt that 3 poor sermons in 30 years was certainly nothing to feel bad about, so he asked her what the $100 was for.

She replied, "Each time I got a dozen eggs, I sold them to the neighbors for $1."

Services

One Sunday morning, pastor Matthews noticed little Alex was staring up at the large plaque that hung in the foyer of the church. The plaque was covered with names, and small American flags were mounted on either side of it. The seven-year-old had been staring at the plaque for some time, so the pastor walked up, stood beside him and said quietly, "Good morning, Alex."

"Good morning, Pastor Matthews," replied the young man, still focused on the plaque. "Pastor Matthews, what is this?" Alex asked.

"Well, son, it's a memorial to all the men and women who have died in the service."

Soberly, they stood together, staring at the large plaque. Little Alex's voice was barely audible when he finally managed to ask, "Which one, the 9:00 or 10:30 service?

Impaired

A humor-impaired preacher attended a conference to help encourage and better equip pastors for their ministry. Among the speakers were many well-known and dynamic speakers.

One "celebrity preacher" boldly approached the pulpit and, gathering the entire crowd's attention, said, "The best years of my life were spent in the arms of a woman that wasn't my wife!" The crowd was shocked! He followed up by saying, "And that woman was my mother!" - The crowd burst into laughter and delivered the rest of his talk, which went over quite well.

The next week, the pastor decided he'd give this humor thing a try, and use that joke in his sermon. As he surely approached the pulpit that sunny Sunday, he tried to rehearse the joke in his head. It suddenly seemed a bit foggy to him.

Getting to the microphone he said loudly, "The greatest years of my life were spent in the arms of another woman that was not my wife!" The congregation inhaled half the air in the room. After standing there for almost 10 seconds in the stunned silence, trying to recall the second half of the joke, the pastor finally blurted out, "...and I can't remember who she was!"

Sermon Prep

Young Zach was watching his father, a pastor, write a sermon." How do you know what to say?" he asked.

"Why, God tells me," answered his father.

"Oh, then why do you keep crossing things out?"

Clarity

At the conclusion of the sermon, the worshipers filed out of the sanctuary to greet the minister, Bill. As one of them left, he shook the minister's hand, thanked him for the sermon and said, "Thanks for the message, Reverend. You know, you must be smarter than Einstein." Beaming with pride, the minister said, "Why, thank you, brother!"

As the week went by, the Bill the minister began to think about the man's compliment. The more he thought, the more he became baffled as to why anyone would deem him smarter than Einstein. So he decided to ask the man the following Sunday.

The next Sunday Bill asked the parishioner if he remembered the previous Sunday's comment about the sermon. The parishioner replied that he did. The minister asked: "Exactly what did you mean that I must be smarter than Einstein?"

The man replied, "Well, Reverend Bill, they say that Einstein was so smart that only ten people in the entire world could understand him. But Reverend, no one can understand you."

Relativity

The clever theology professor was taking it easy, lying on the grass and looking up at the clouds. He was identifying shapes when he decided to talk to God. "God", he said, "how long is a million years?"

God answered, "In my frame of reference, it's about a minute."

The professor asked, "God, how much is a million dollars?"

God answered, "To Me, it's a penny."

The professor then asked, "God, can I have a penny?"

God said, "In a minute."

Creator

One day a group of scientists got together and decided that humans had come a long way and no longer needed God. So they picked one scientist to go and tell God that they were done with worshiping the Divine.

The scientist walked up to God and said, "God, we've decided that we no longer need you. We're to the point that we can clone people and do many miraculous things, so why don't you just go on and get lost."

God listened very patiently and kindly to the man. After the scientist was done talking, God said, "Very well, how about this?

Let's say we have a human-making contest." To which the scientist replied, "Okay, great!"

But God added, "Now, we're going to do this just like I did back in the old days with Adam."

The scientist said, "Sure, no problem" and bent down and grabbed himself a handful of dirt.

God looked at him and said, "No, no, no. You go get your own dirt!"

Longevity

God created the donkey and told him: you will work tireless from sun up to sun down, carrying heavy bags on your back, you'll eat grass, you will not have intelligence and you will live 50 years. You will be a DONKEY!

The donkey answered: I'll be a donkey, but living 50 years is too much, give me only 20 years. And God gave the donkey 20 years.

God created the dog and told him: You will look after the man's house, you will be his best friend, you will eat whatever they give you and you will live 25 years. You will be a DOG!

The dog answered: God, living 25 years is too much, give only 10. God gave the dog 10 years.

God created the monkey and told him: You will jump from branch to branch, you will do silly things, you will be amusing and you will live 20 years.

The monkey answered: God, living 20 years is too much, give me only 10 years. And God agreed.

Finally, God created humans, and told them: You will be Human, the only rational being on this earth, you will use your intelligence to control other animals, you will dominate the world and you will live for 20 years.

The humans answered: God, we'll be human, but living 20 years is not enough, why don't you give us the 30 years that the donkey refused, the 20 years that the dog did not want and the 10 years that the monkey refused.

That was what God did, and since then, humans live 20 years like a human being, then they enter adulthood and spend 30 years like a donkey, working and carrying the load on their backs, then when their children leave home, spend 15 years like a dog, looking after the house and eating whatever is given to them, then they get into retirement, and spend 10 years like a monkey, jumping from house to house or from children to children, doing silly things to amuse the grandchildren.

Pets

A newly discovered chapter in the Book of Genesis has provided the answer to "Where do pets come from?" Adam said, "Lord, when I was in the garden, you walked with me every day. Now I do not see you anymore. I am lonesome here and it is difficult for me to remember how much you love me."

And God said, "No problem! I will create a companion for you that will be with you forever and who will be a reflection of my love for you, so that you will love me even when you cannot see me. Regardless of how selfish or childish or unlovable you may be, this new companion will accept you as you are and will love you as I do, in spite of yourself."

And God created a new animal to be a companion for Adam. And it was a good animal. And God was pleased. And the new animal was pleased to be with Adam and he wagged his tail. And Adam said, "Lord, I have already named all the animals in the Kingdom and I cannot think of a name for this new animal."

And God said, "No problem! Because I have created this new animal to be a reflection of my love for you, his name will be a reflection of my own name, and you will call him DOG."

And Dog lived with Adam and was a companion to him and loved him. And Adam was comforted. And God was pleased. And Dog was content and wagged his tail.

After a while, it came to pass that Adam's guardian angel came to the Lord and said, "Lord, Adam has become filled with pride. He struts and preens like a peacock and he believes he is worthy of adoration. Dog has indeed taught him that he is loved, but perhaps too well."

And the Lord said, "No problem! I will create for him a companion who will be with him forever and who will see him as he is. The companion will remind him of his limitations, so he will know that he is not always worthy of adoration."

And God created Cat to be a companion to Adam. And Cat would not obey Adam. And when Adam gazed into Cat's eyes, he was reminded that he was not the supreme being. And Adam learned humility.

And God was pleased.
And Adam was greatly improved.
And Dog was happy.
And the Cat didn't give a hoot one way or the other.

Made in the USA
Middletown, DE
08 April 2018